Ancaster and Mount Hope Ontario in Photos, Saving Our History One Photo at a Time

Photography
by Barbara Raué
2012-2013

Series Name:
Cruising Ontario

Book 16: Ancaster and Mount Hope

Cover photo: St. John's Anglican Church,
272 Wilson Street East, Ancaster

Series Name: Cruising Ontario

Book 1: London
Book 2: Dundas
Book 3: Hamilton
Book 4: Oakville
Book 5: Chesley
Book 6: Stoney Creek
Book 7: Waterdown
Book 8: Owen Sound
Book 9: Mount Forest
Book 10: Dundalk
Book 11: Burford and Area
Book 12: Waterford and Area
Book 13: Drumbo and Area
Book 14: Sheffield and Area
Book 15: Tavistock and Area
Book 16: Ancaster and Mount Hope

Other Books by Barbara Raue

Coins and Gems

Arrows, Indians and Love

The Life and Times of Barbara
Volume 1: Inventions That Have Enhanced My Life
Volume 2: Entertainment That I Have Enjoyed
Volume 3: East Coast Trips
Volume 4: Olympics
Volume 5: Wonders of the World
Volume 6: Caribbean Cruises

Ancaster

A wooden grist mill and sawmill was constructed here in 1791-92 by millwright James Wilson with financial backing from Richard Beasley. This was the start of the settlement of Ancaster in 1793. Wilson sold his interest in the mills and some adjoining land in 1794 to Jean Baptiste Rouseaux who expanded the commercial activity of the village by building a general store, brewery and hotel. After the War of 1812, the Egleston brothers built a farm equipment foundry; Job Lodor built a woollen mill; Eyre Thuresson built a threshing machine factory (now converted to a home); and Jasper Crane built an impressive stone four-storey knitting mill (1854-1875).

Ancaster became part of the amalgamated City of Hamilton in 2001.

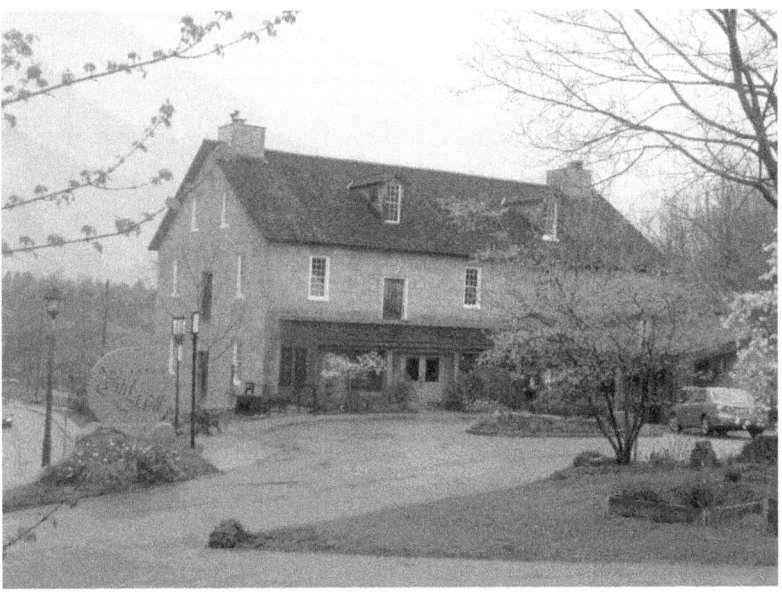

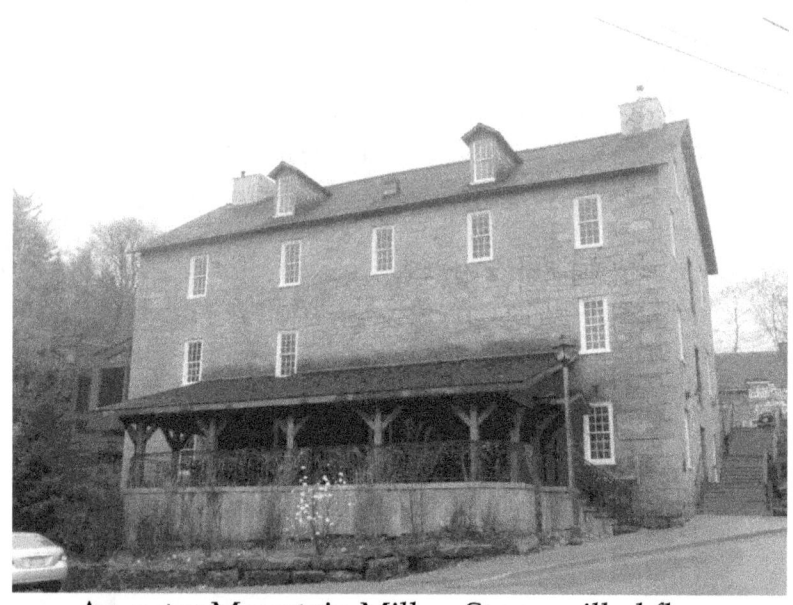

Ancaster Mountain Mills – Stone milled flour

The Ancaster Mill is one of the few remaining operating grist mills in Ontario. The original mill built south of Wilson Street in 1791 was destroyed by fire at the onset of the War of 1812 and replaced 300 yards downstream. The second mill burned and was replaced in 1818 on the present site. In 1854 this mill burned and was replaced by the present structure in 1863. The building is constructed of solid limestone walls with decorative corner quoins. The gable roof has two gabled-dormers on each side and the double-hung windows have flared stone lintels.

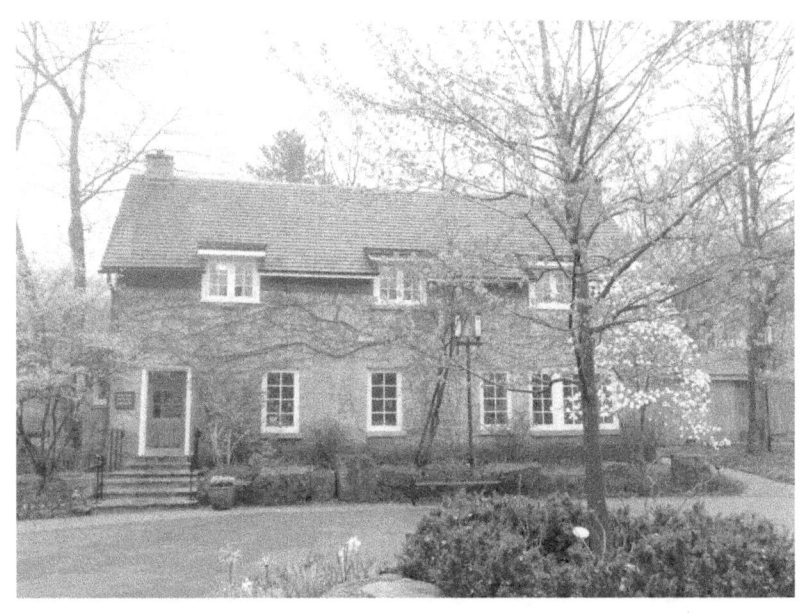

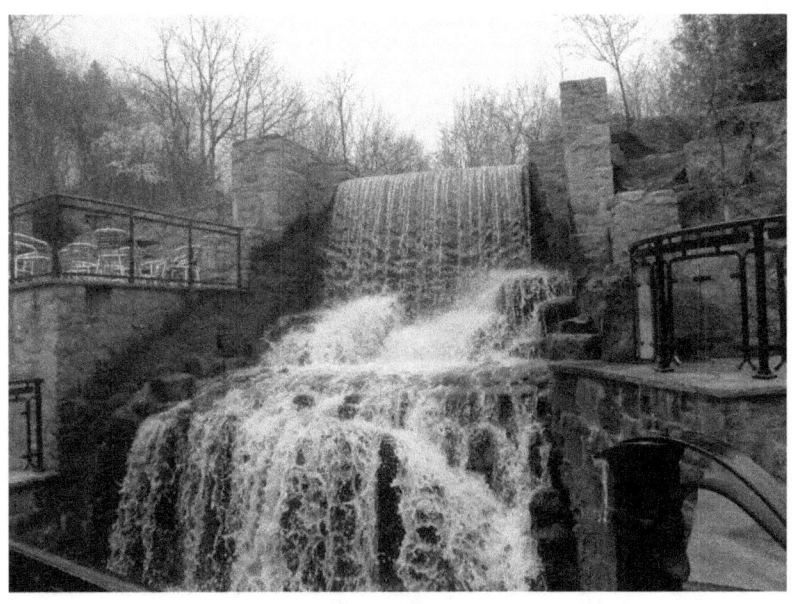

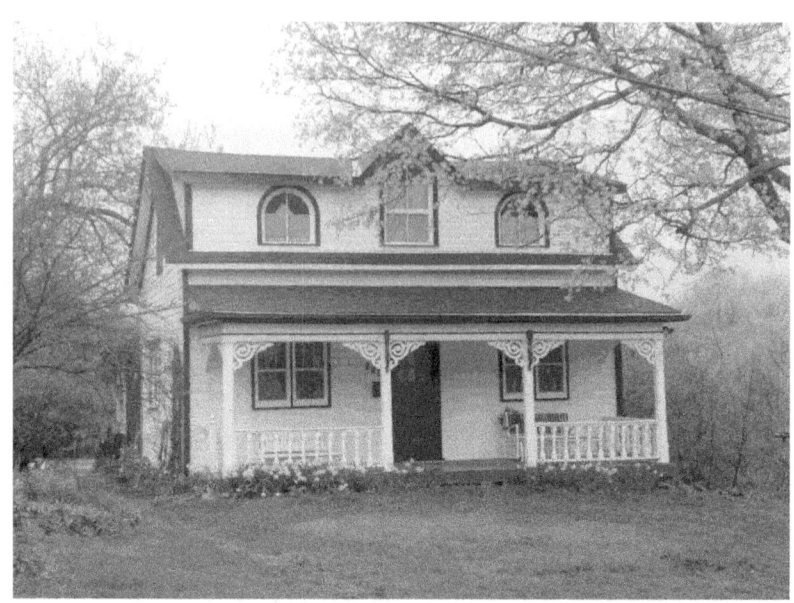

Gothic Revival style with centre gable

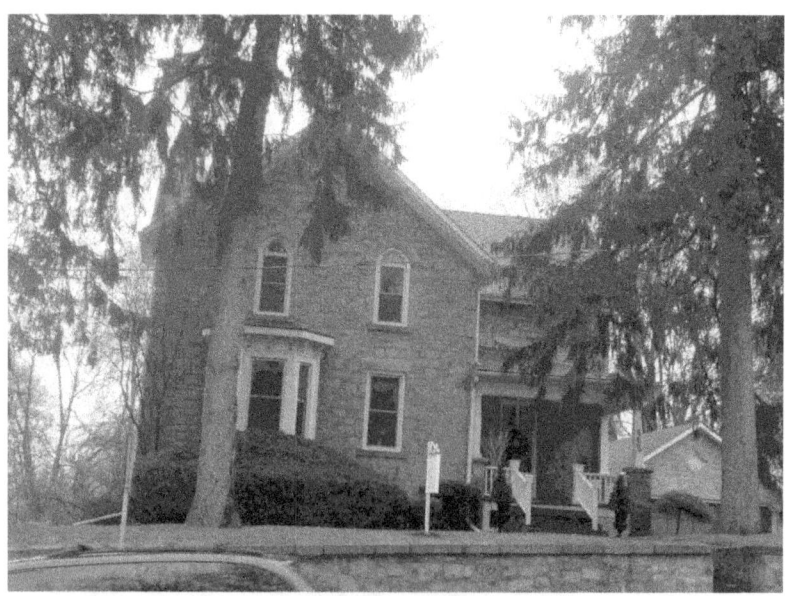

The Brandon House – 462 Wilson Street East

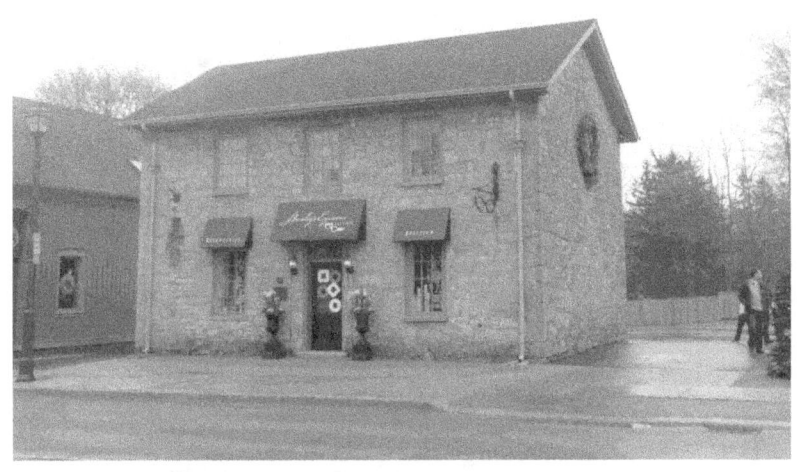

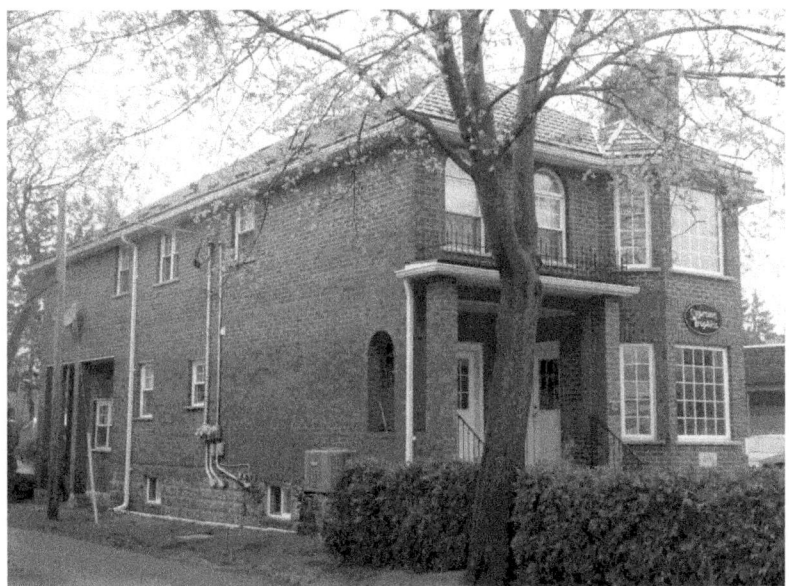

401 Wilson Street East

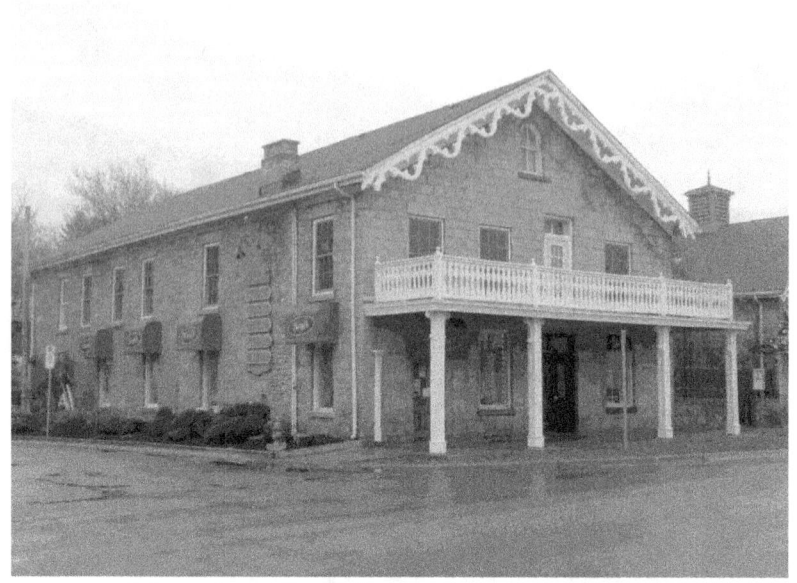

Limestone building, gingerbread trim

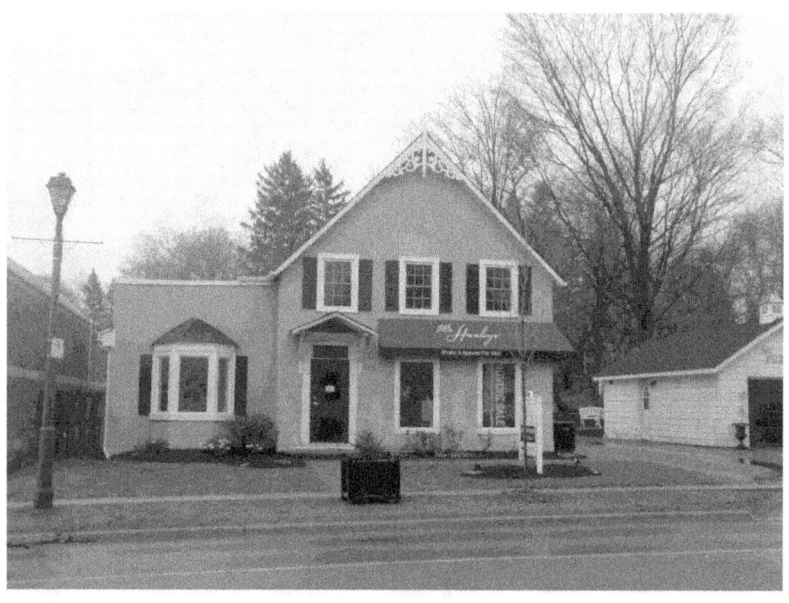

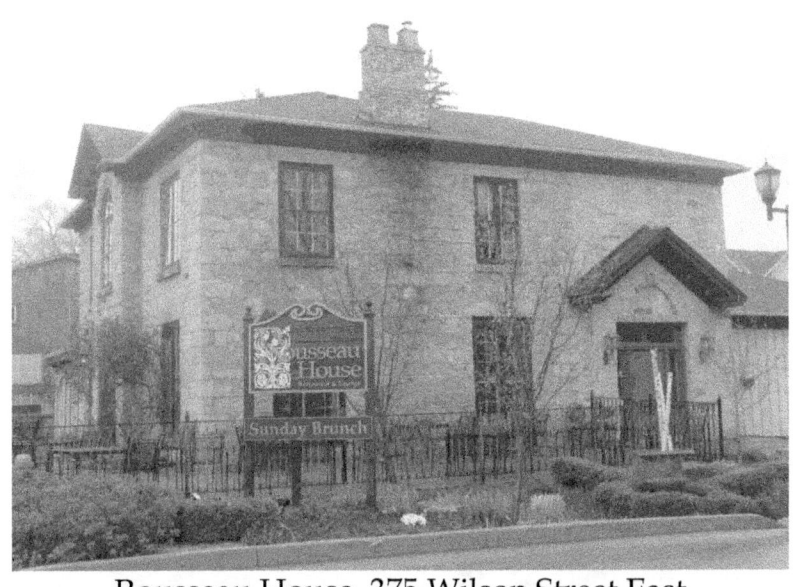

Rousseau House, 375 Wilson Street East
The house was built in 1838 by George Brock Rousseau,
postmaster of Ancaster for ten years.

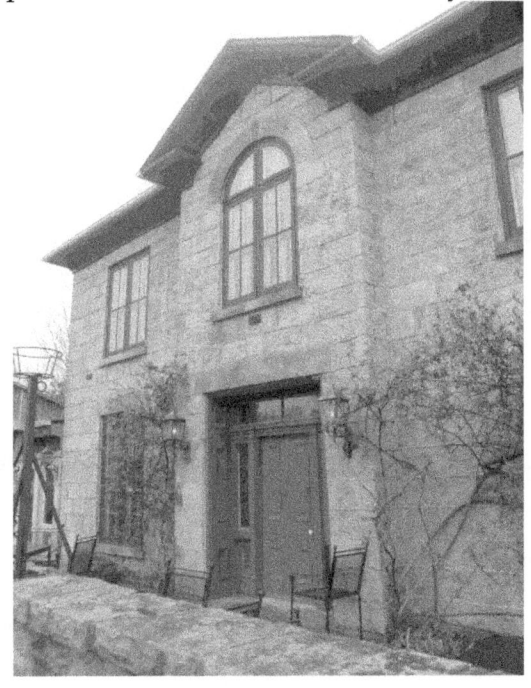

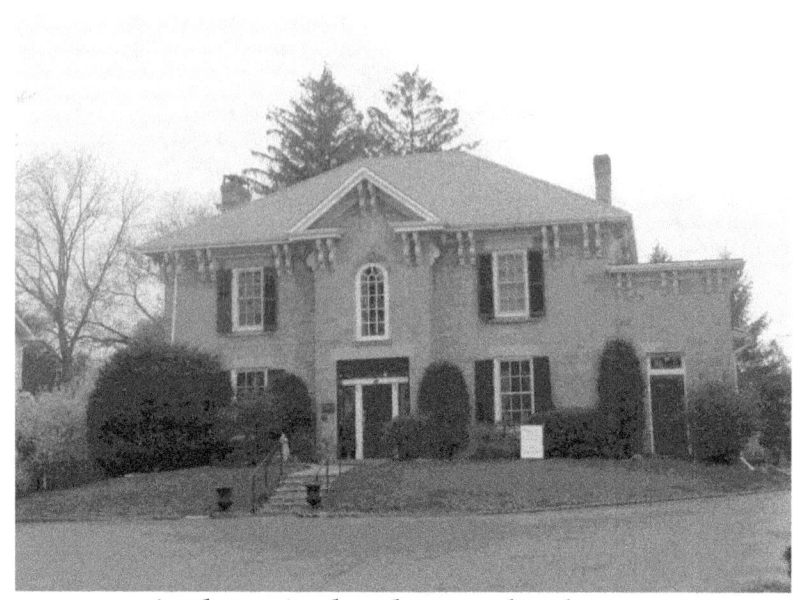

paired cornice brackets under the eaves

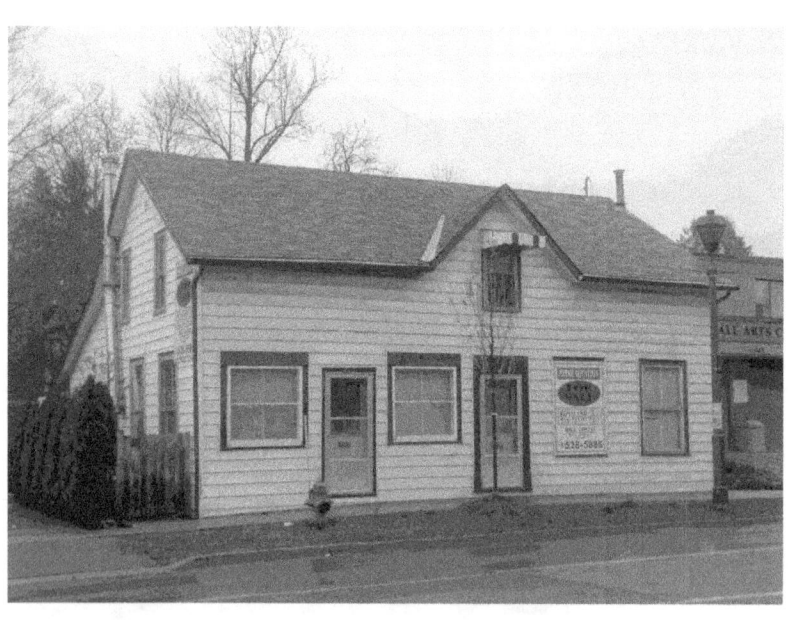

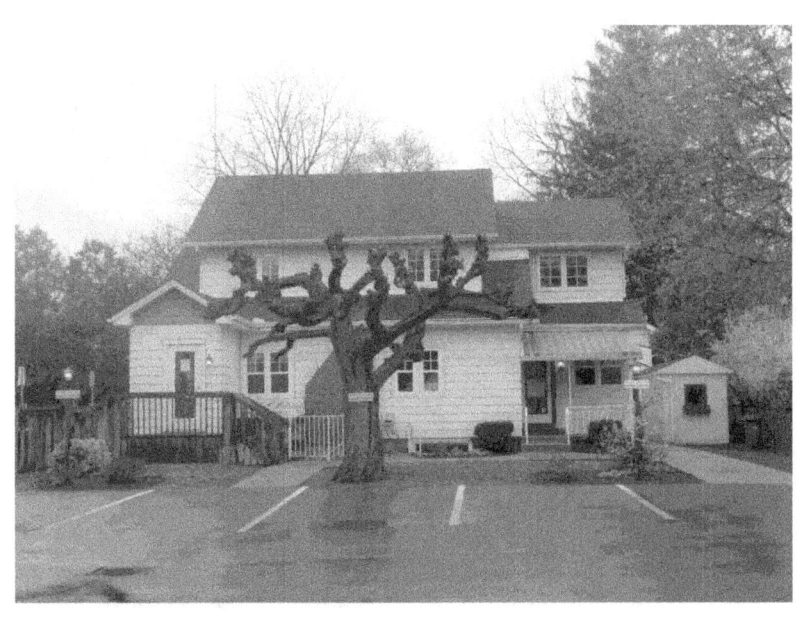

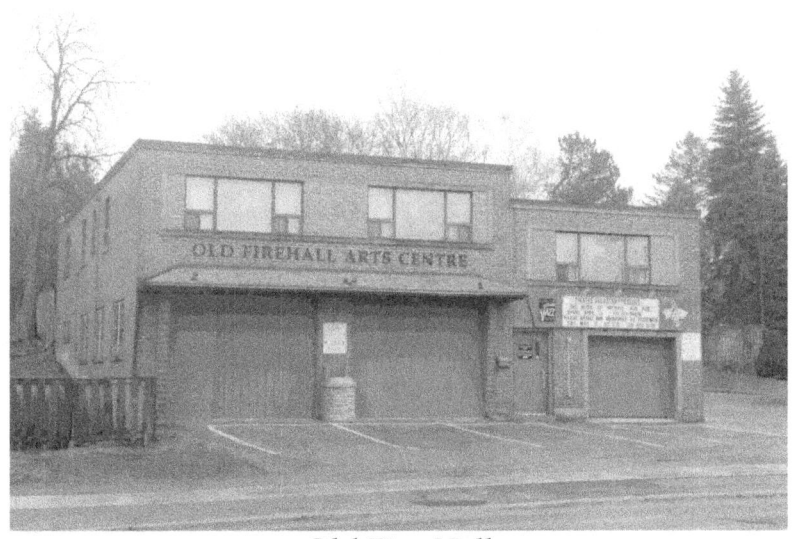

Old Fire Hall

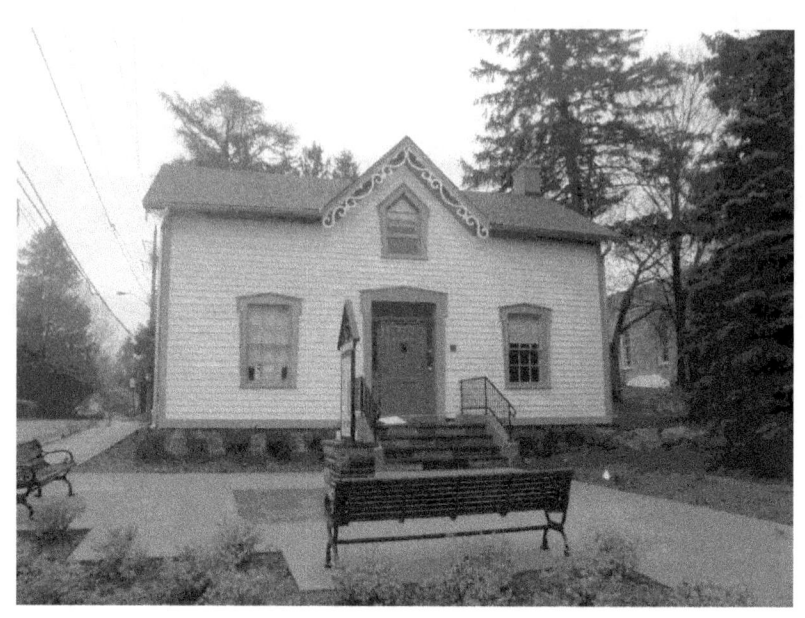

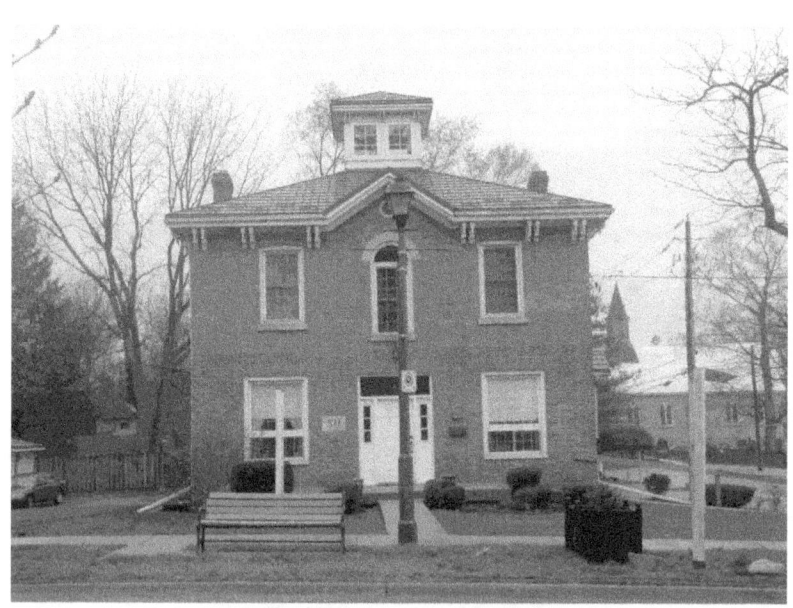

311 Wilson Street East

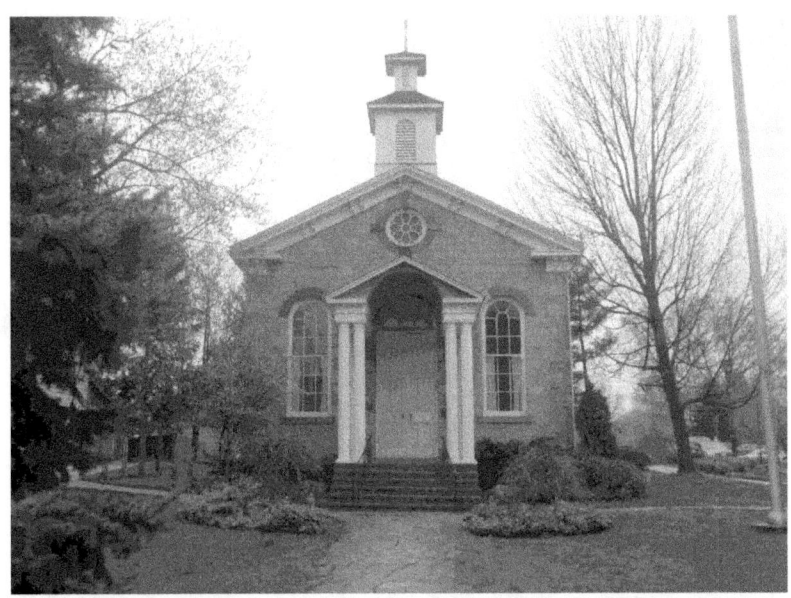

Township Hall was constructed in 1871, a stone building in the Georgian style of architecture with a neo-classical portico and an Italianate cupola.

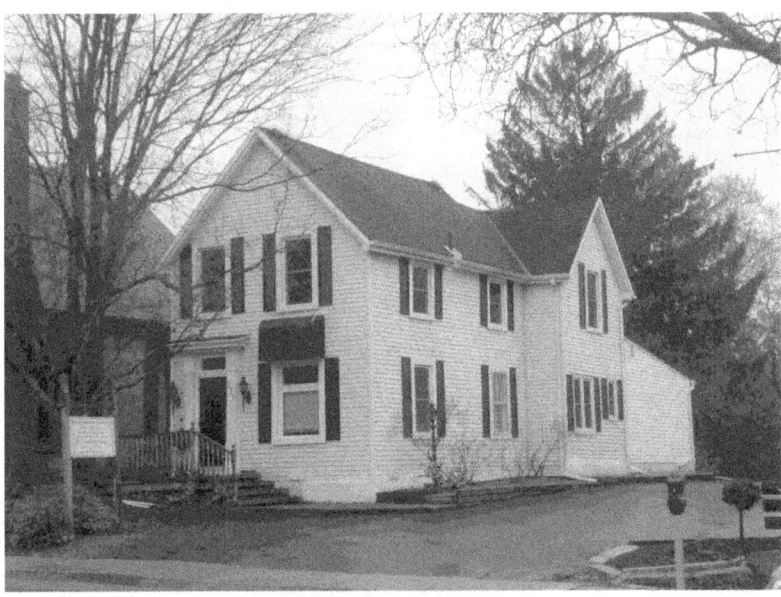

277 Wilson Street

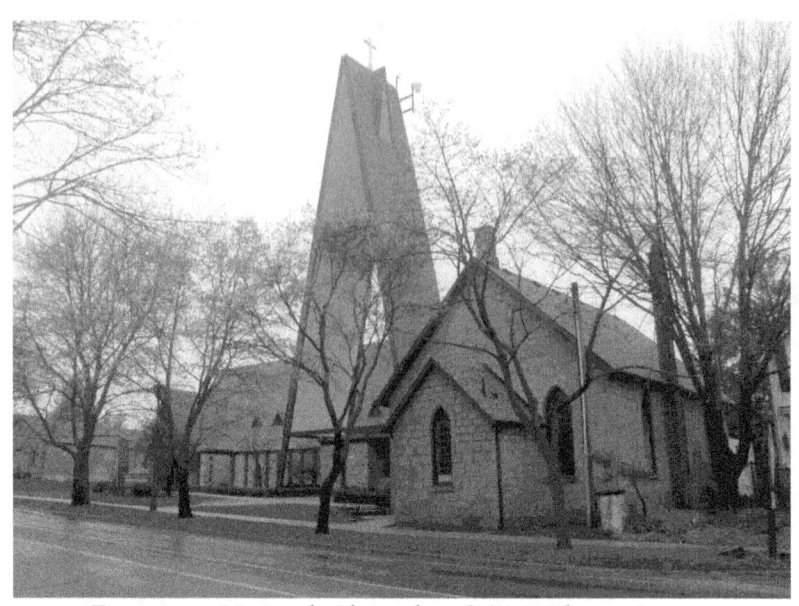

Ryerson United Church – 265 Wilson Street

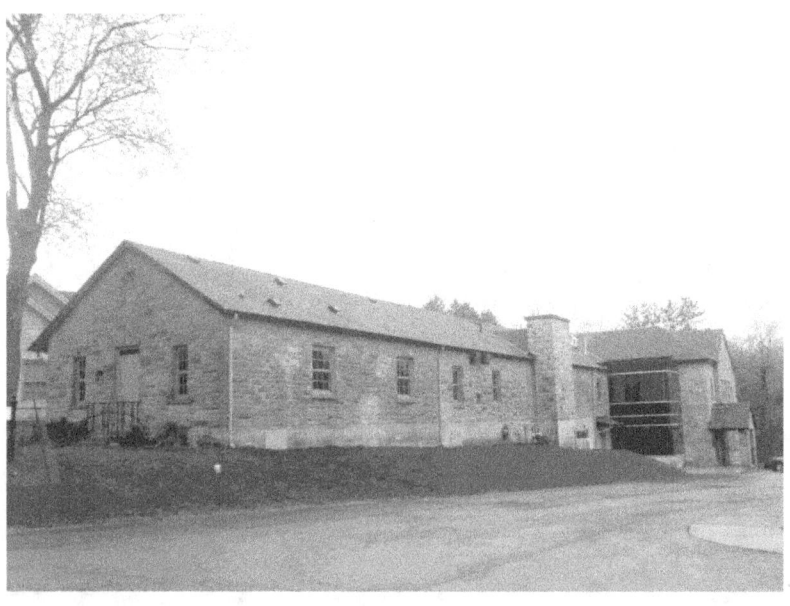

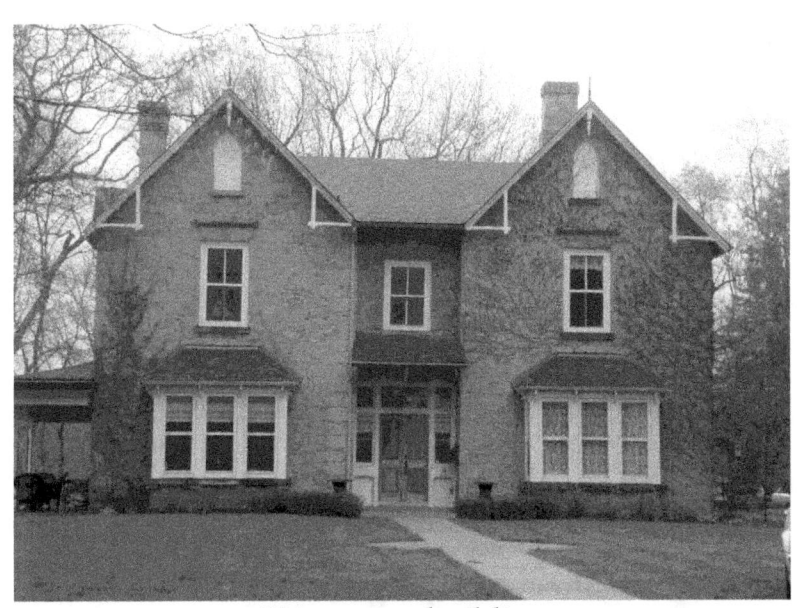

#21 – stone building

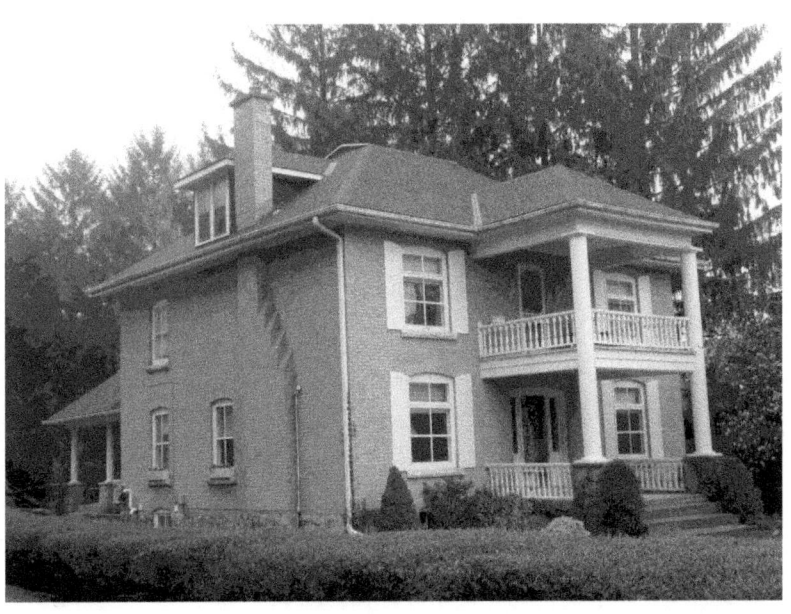

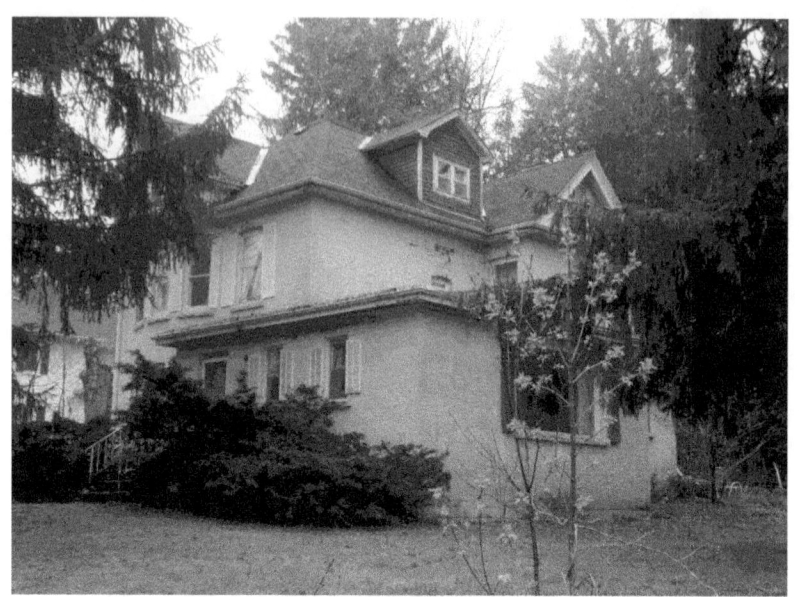

#16

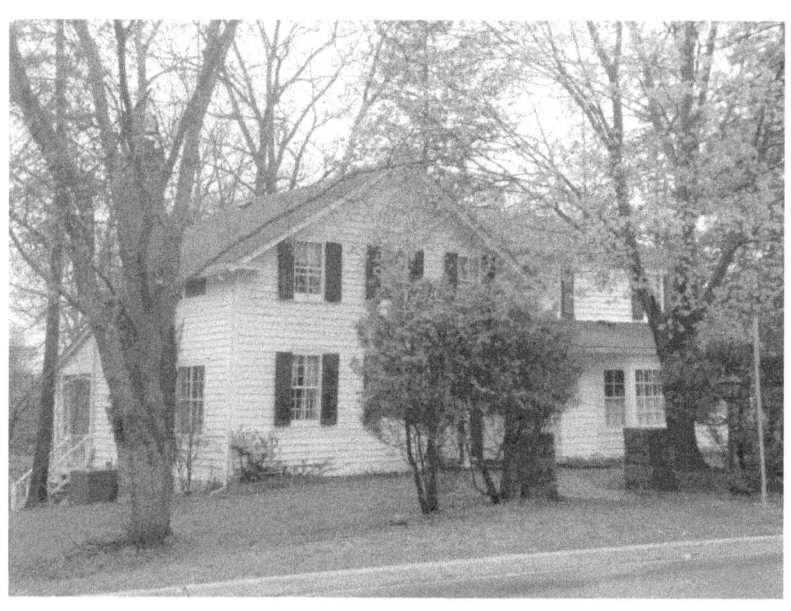

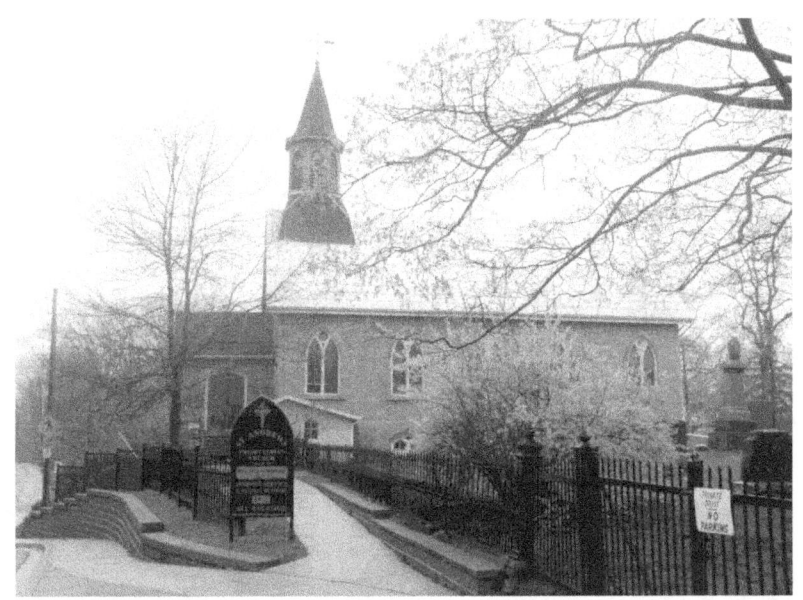

St. Andrews Presbyterian Church, 31 Sulphur Springs Road
Founded in 1826 – present stone building completed in 1875

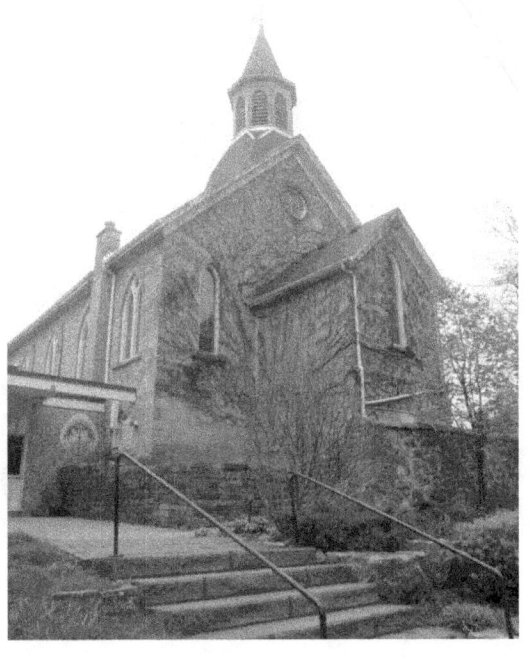

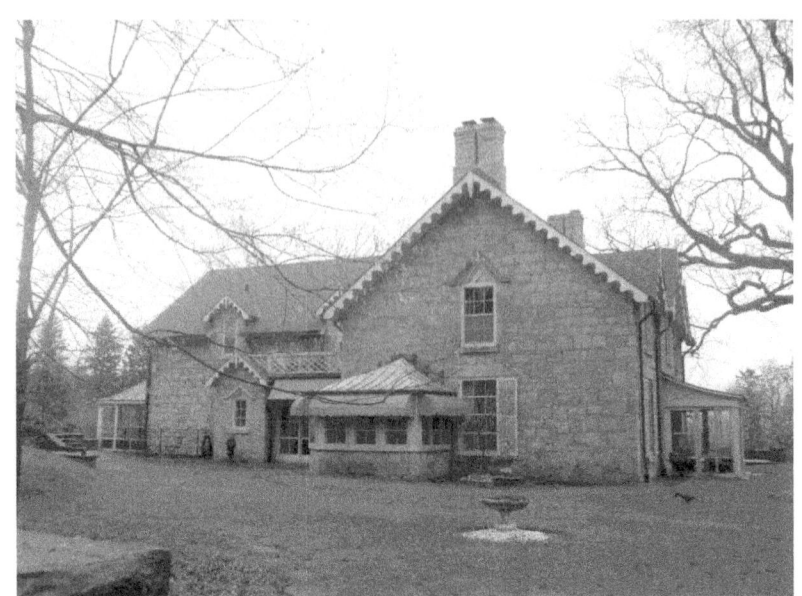

Fairview

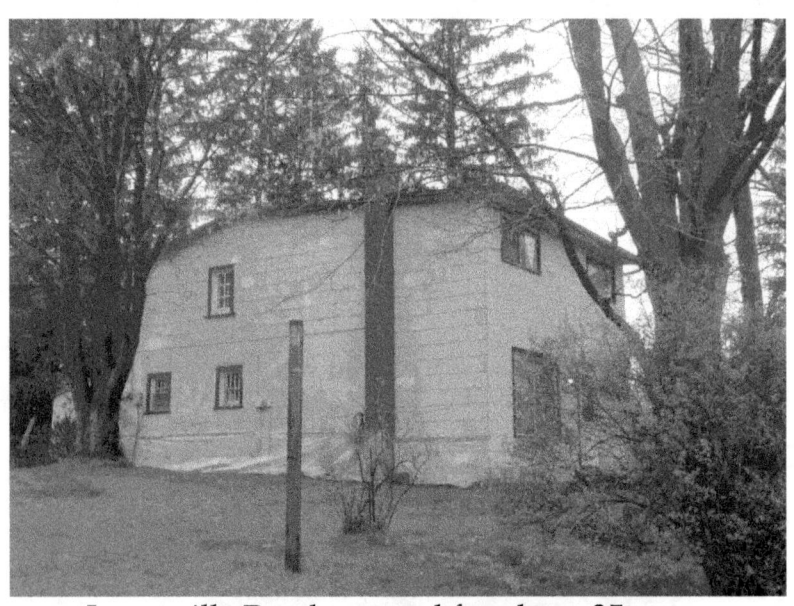

Jerseyville Road – rented for about 35 years
by Klaus and Judy Brandt

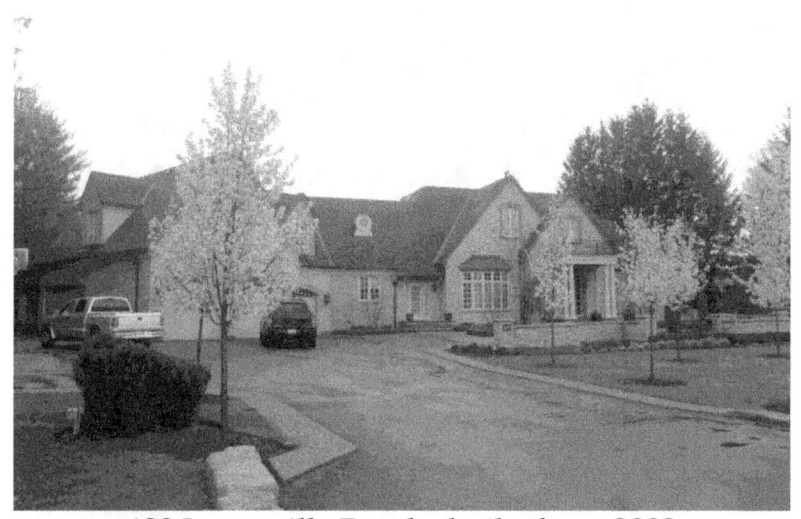

489 Jerseyville Road – built about 2008

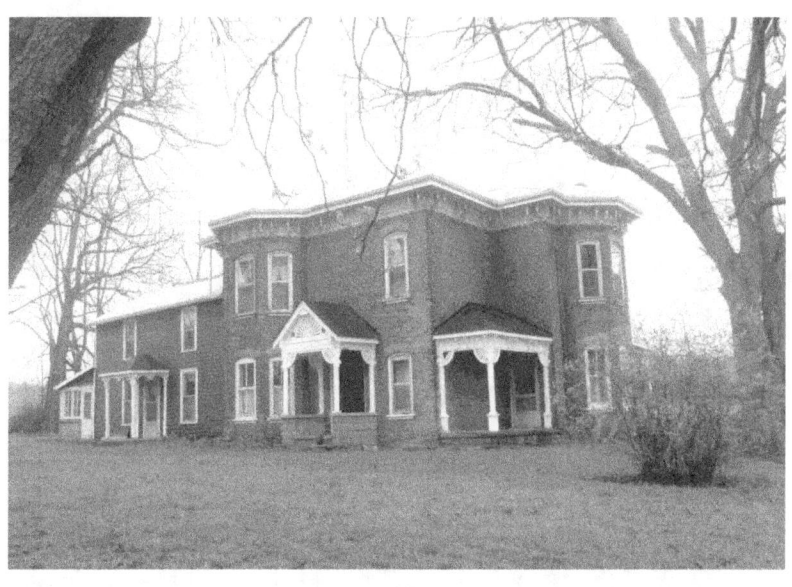

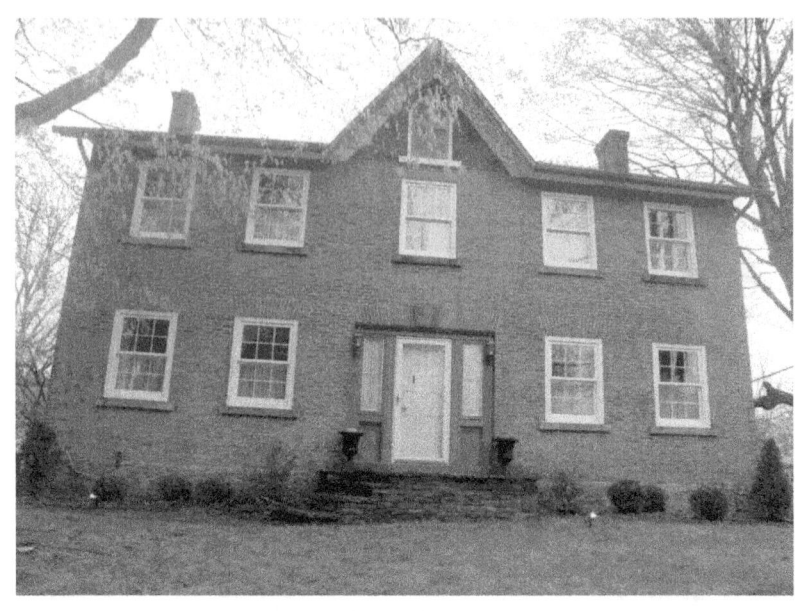

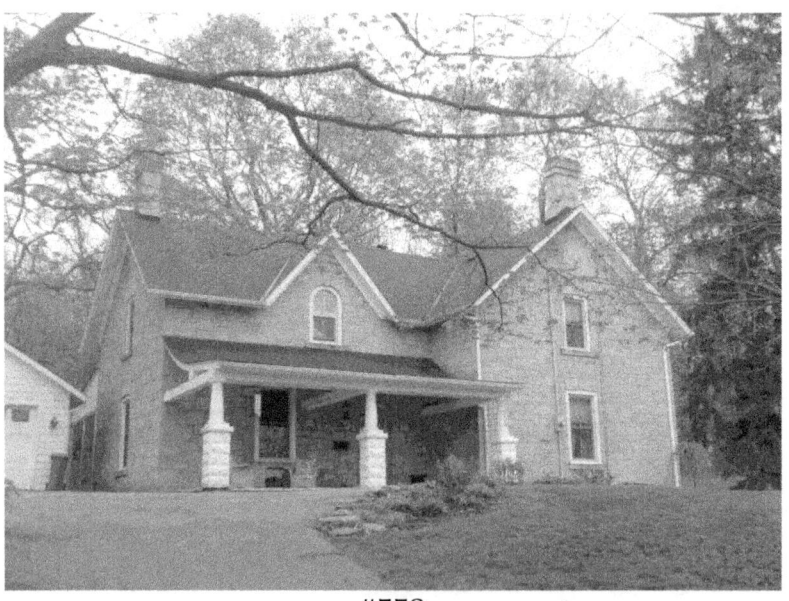

#558

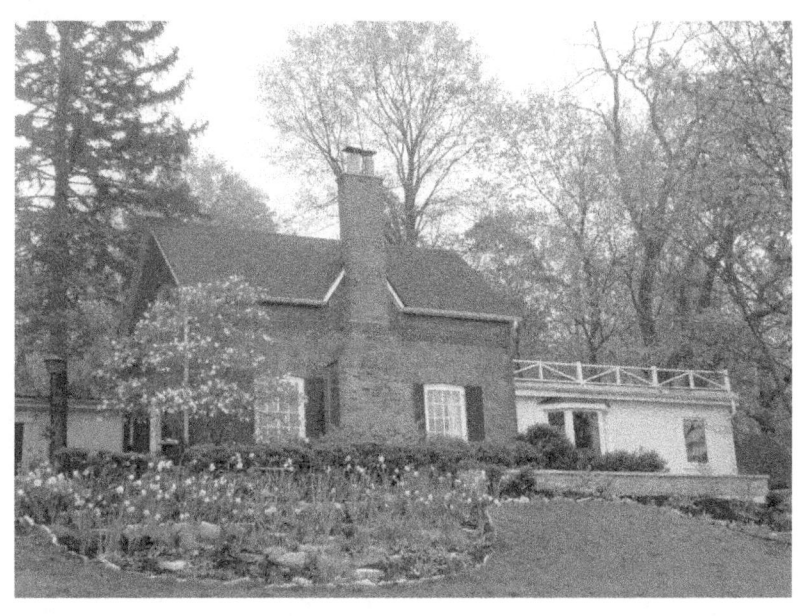

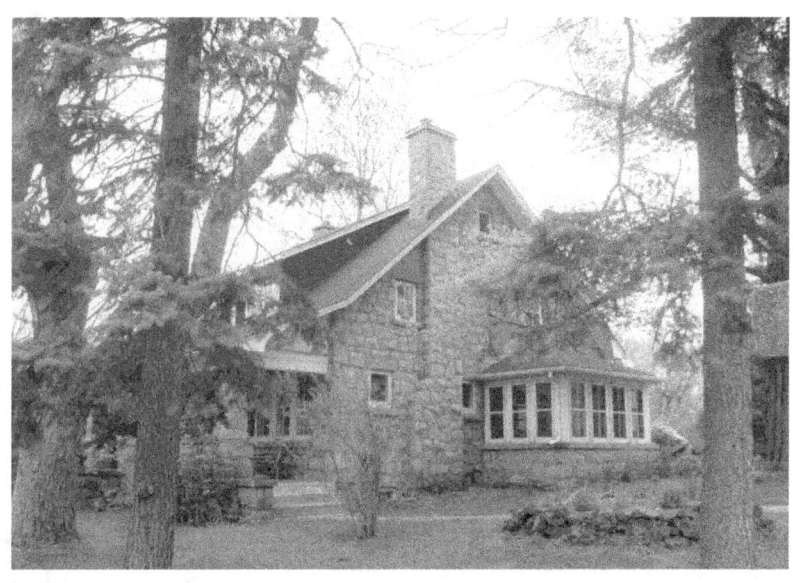

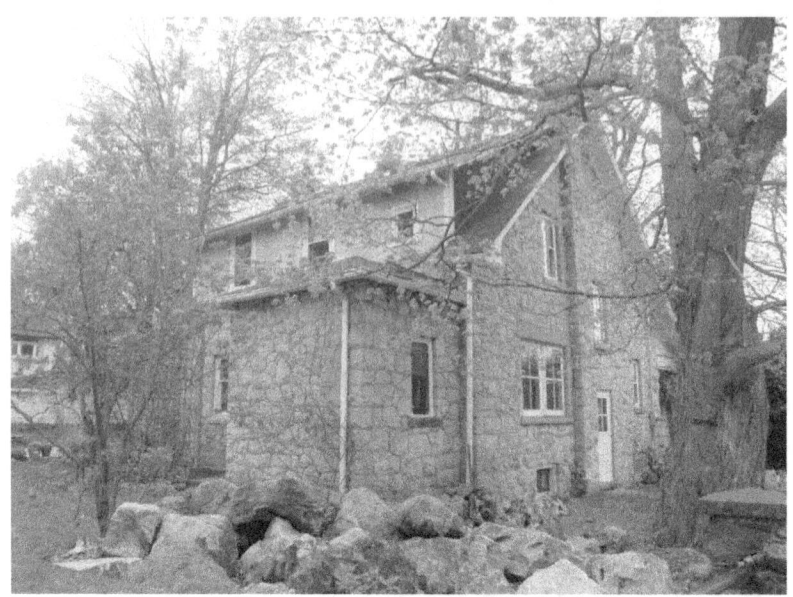

Stone building

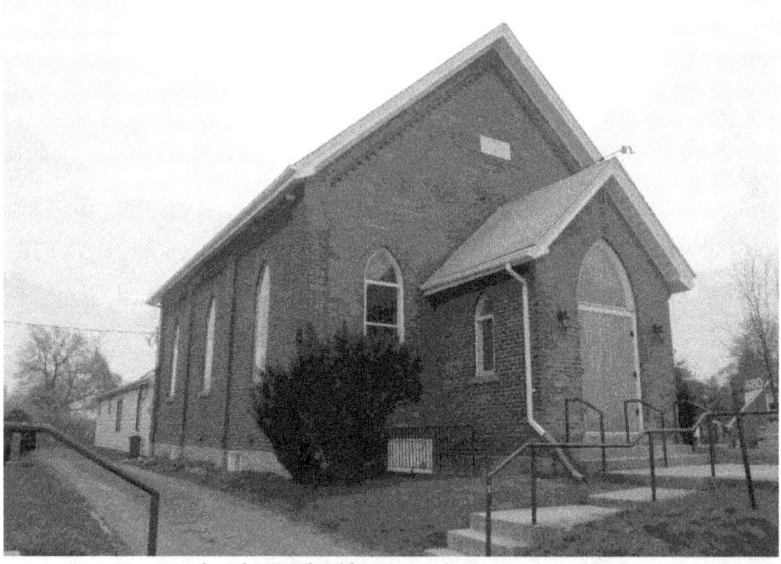

Bowman United Church (formerly Methodist – circa 1796)
Joined the United Church in 1925 - 880 Garner Road East

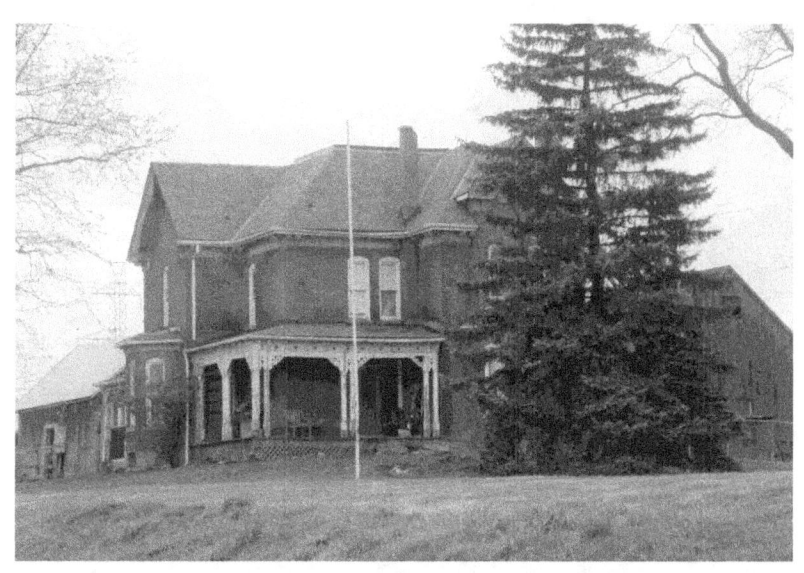

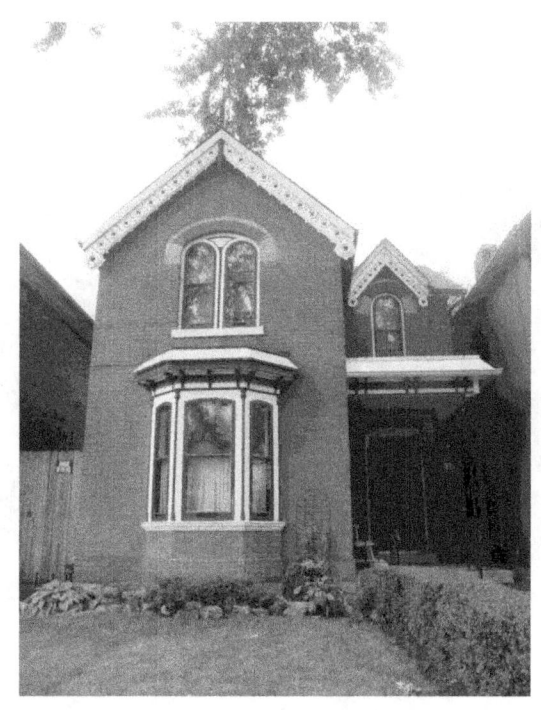

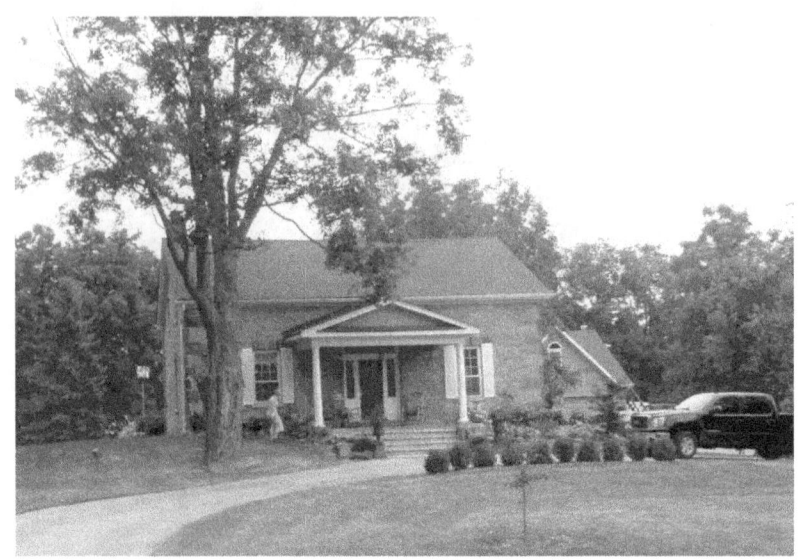

Garner Road East

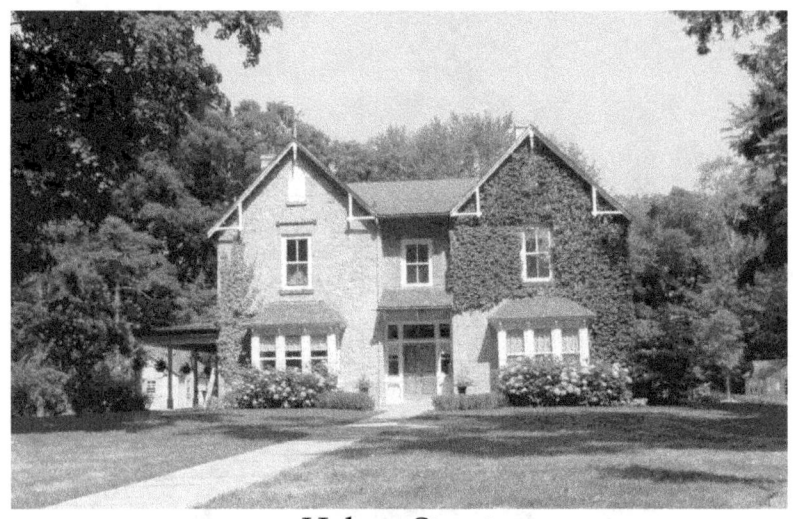

Halson Street

Mount Hope

Mount Hope is one of the six communities forming The City of Hamilton since its amalgamation in 2001.

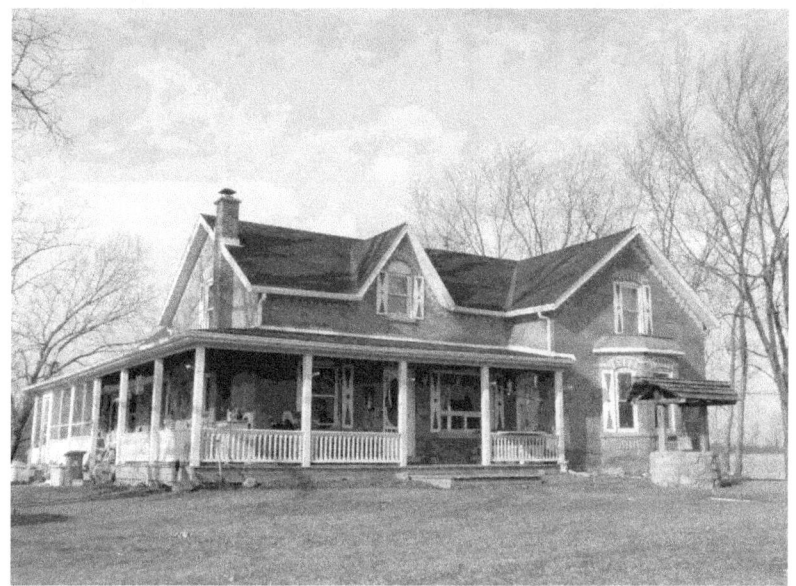

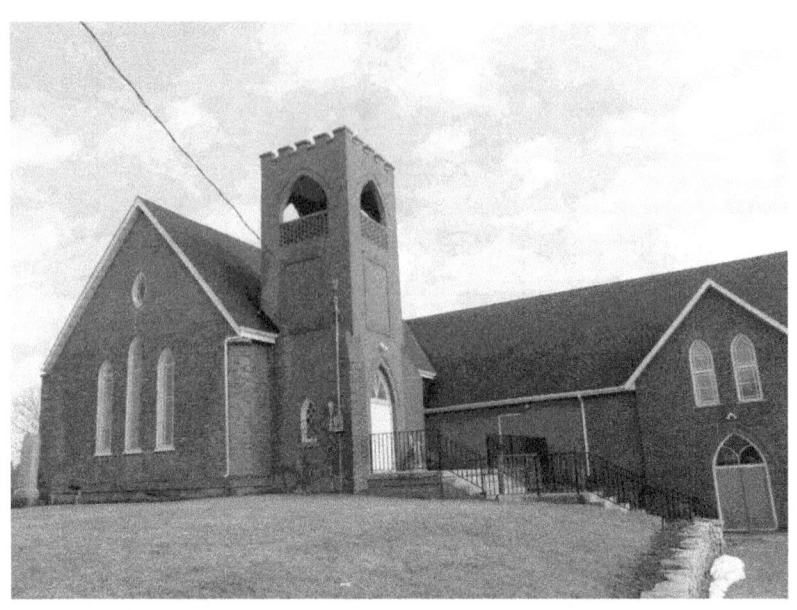

St. Paul's Anglican Church, Glanford

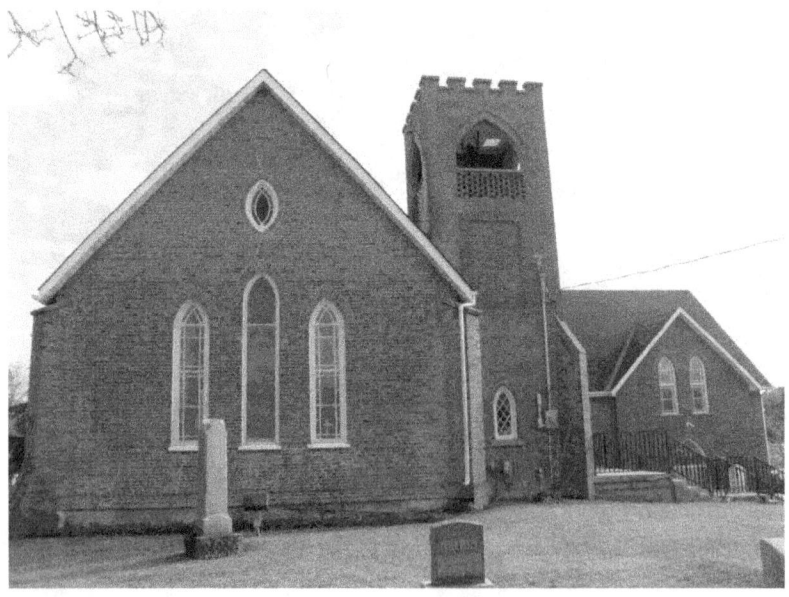

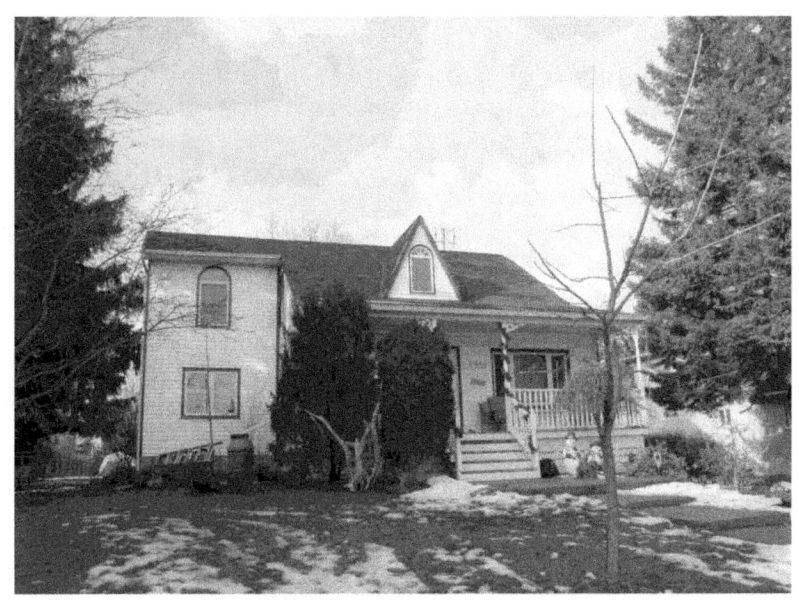

2958 Homestead Drive

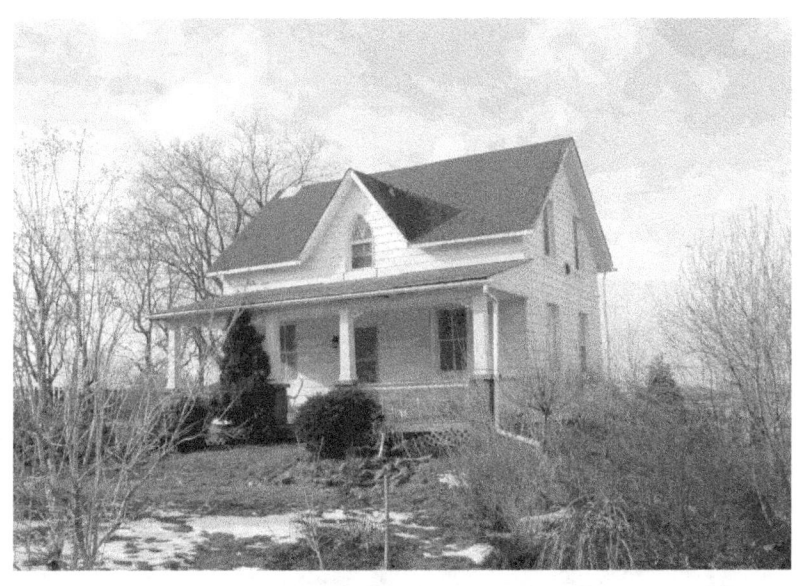

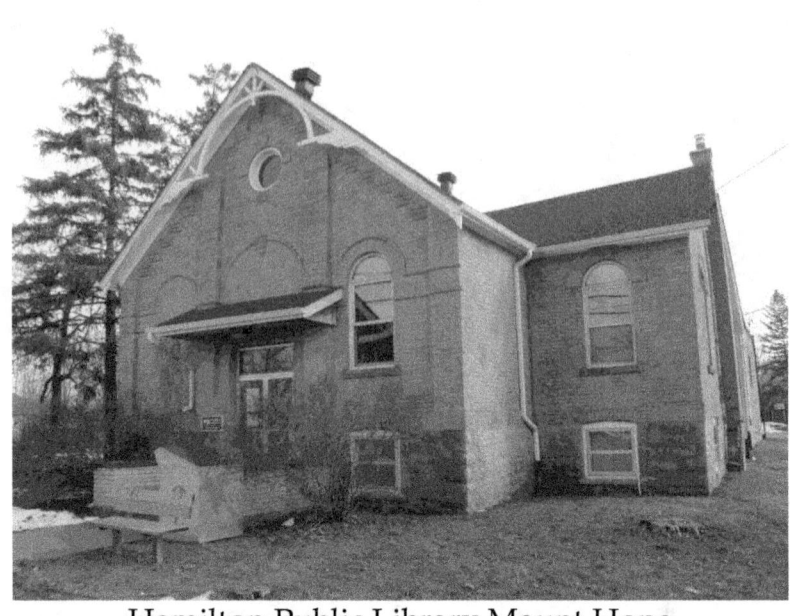

Hamilton Public Library Mount Hope
3027 Homestead Drive
In 1990, the former administrative offices of the Township of
Glanbrook were renovated for use as a library.

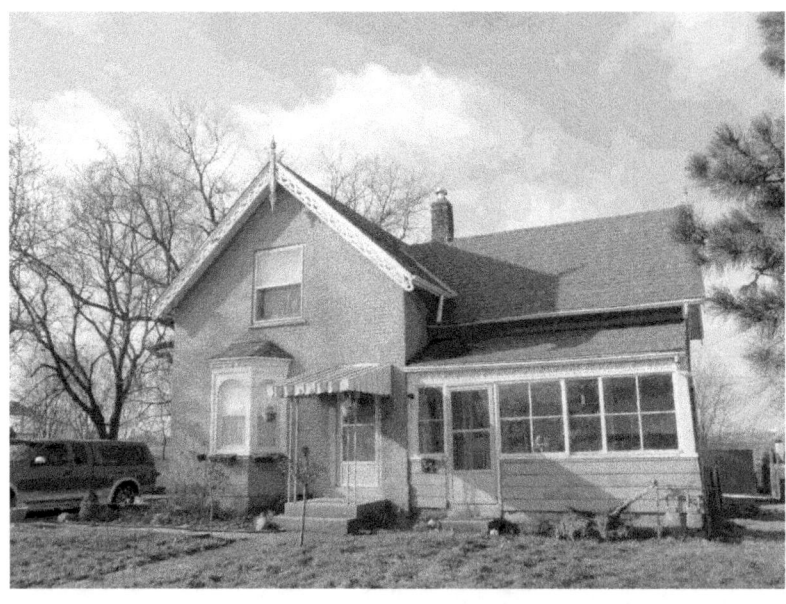

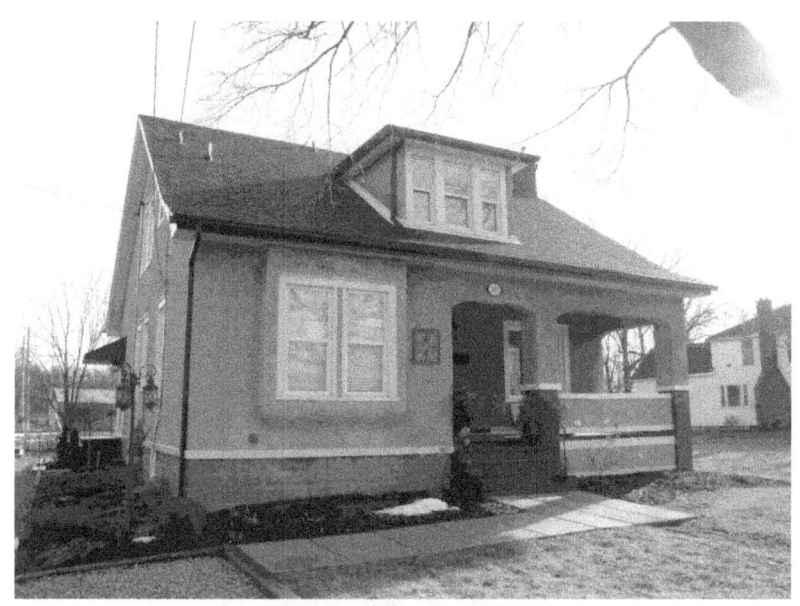

Stucco home #3041

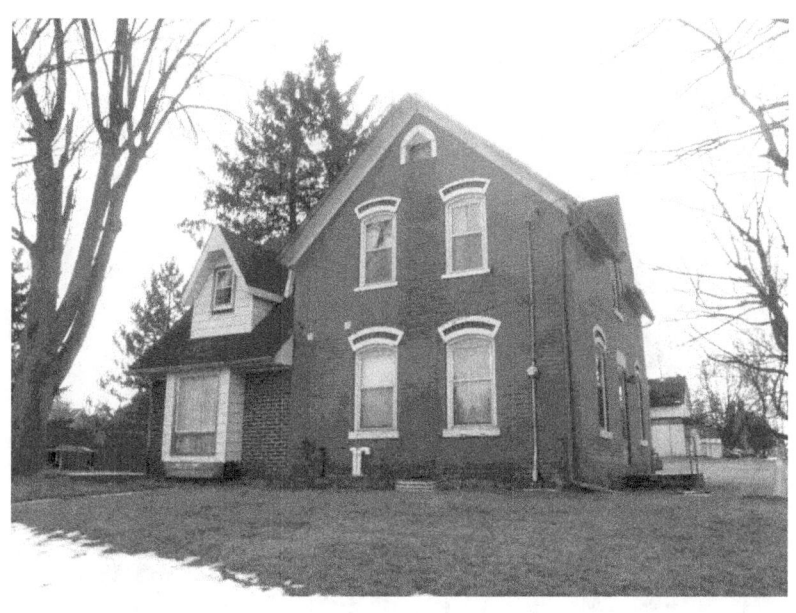

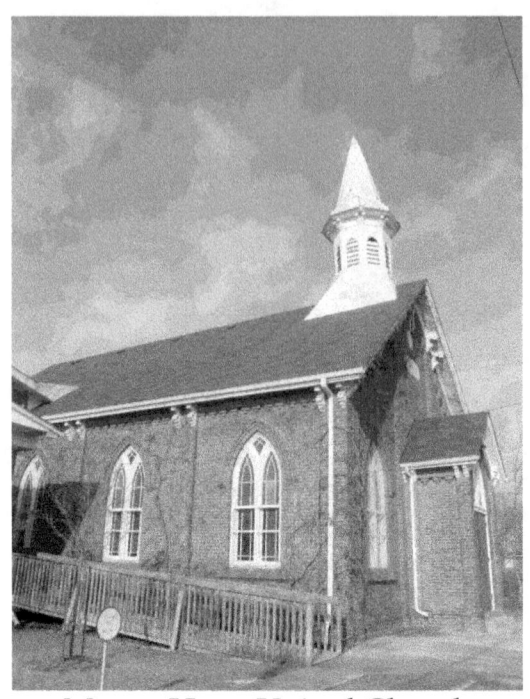

Mount Hope United Church
3076 Homestead Drive

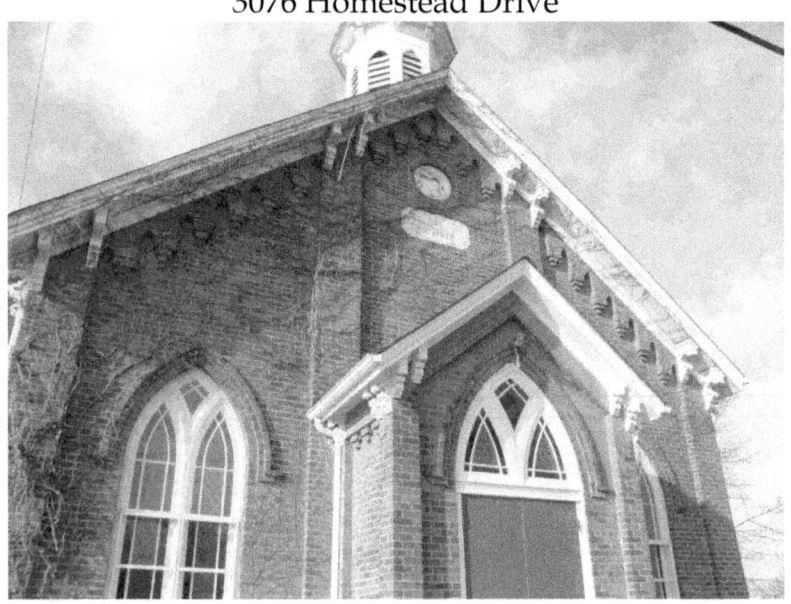

John C. Munro Hamilton International Airport, 9300 Airport Road, Mount Hope, was built in October 1940 as a wartime air force training station for flight training, air navigation, telegraphy, and air gunnery. After World War II, the airport became a public facility.

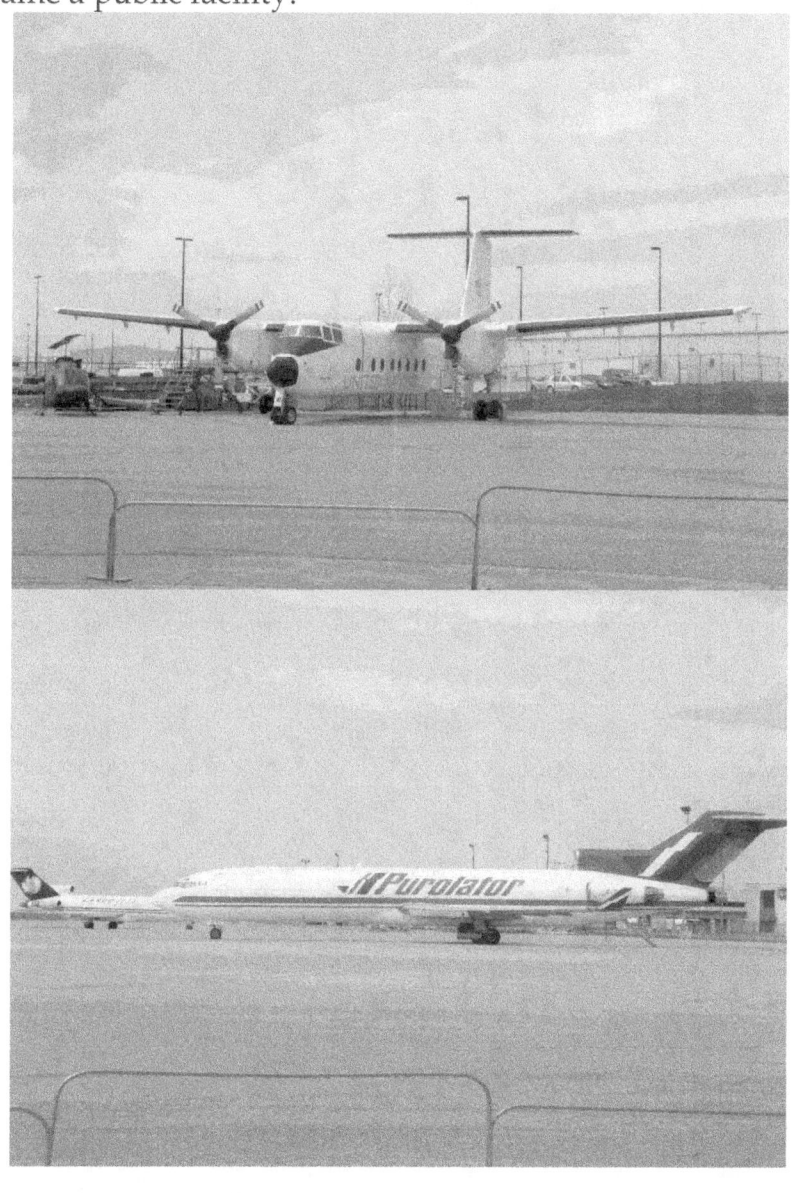

Canadian Warplane Heritage Museum, Mount Hope, with over 25 aircraft in flying condition, features the aircraft used by Canadians and the Canadian Military from the beginning of World War II to the present.

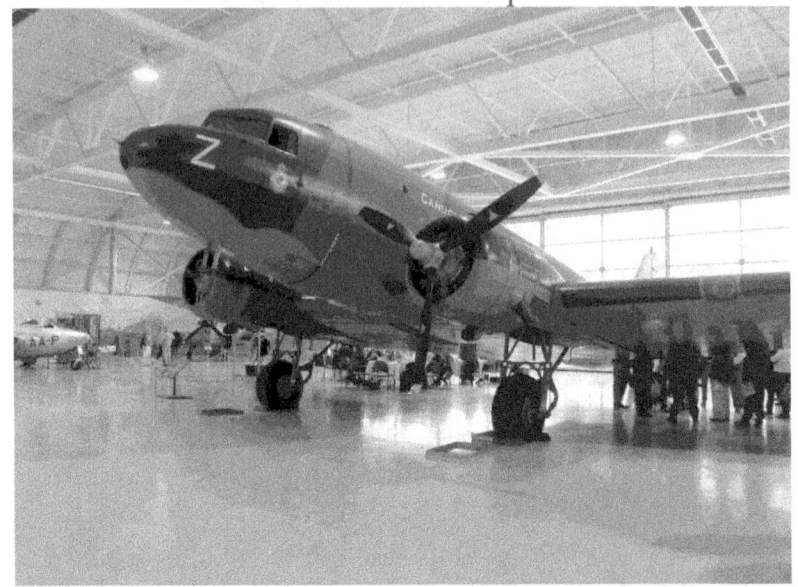

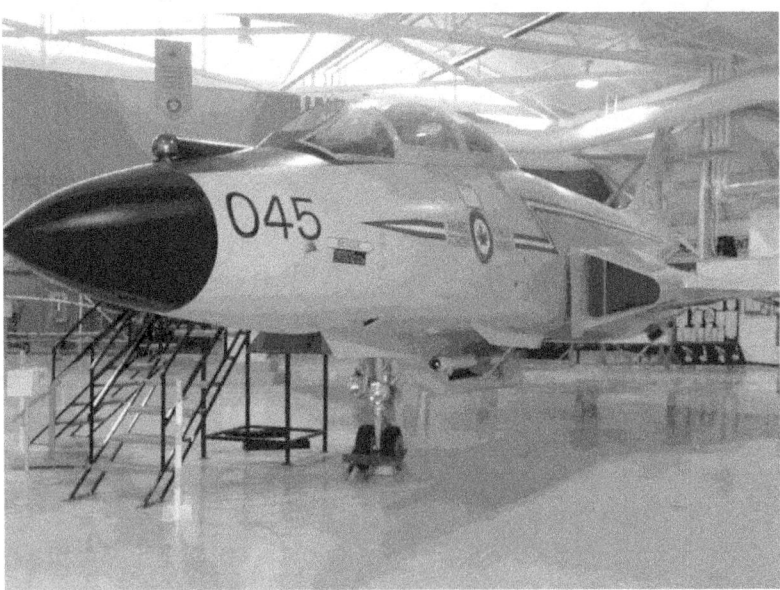

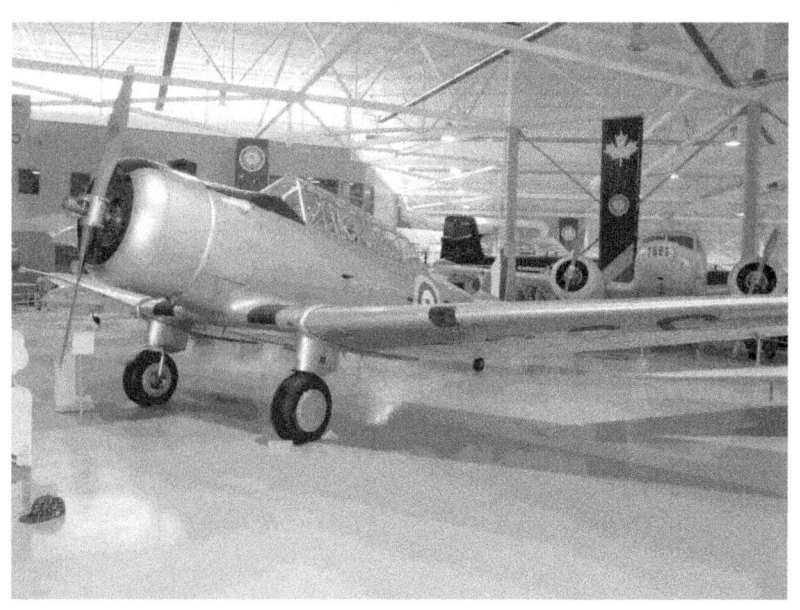

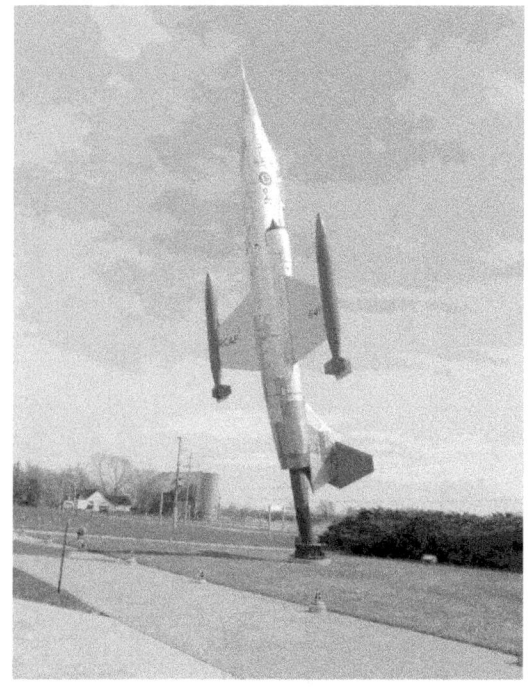